Transformed by GRACE

52 MORE PRAYERS IN THE WESLEYAN SPIRIT

PAUL W. CHILCOTE

UPPER ROOM BOOKS®
NASHVILLE

Transformed by Grace: 52 More Prayers in the Wesleyan Spirit

Cover design: Bruce Gore
Interior design and typesetting: PerfecType | Nashville, TN

ISBN: 978-0-8358-2070-7
Epub ISBN: 978-0-8358-2071-4

For more information on resources available from The Upper Room call 1-800-972-0433 or visit www.upperroom.org

For all United Methodists
and others within the Wesleyan family
who see a future filled with hope

Contents

Preface

Translating John Wesley's sermons into forms of prayer has been an important spiritual discipline for me. Wesley's sermons are filled with deep spiritual wisdom, and I have gained so many important insights through that process of converting proclamation into prayer. Likewise, I have used the hymns of Charles Wesley devotionally for years. They never cease to challenge and inspire me. The hymns provide an opportunity, not just to meditate upon, but to sing about God's love and our life with Christ. To sing is to pray twice. This proclaimed and sung faith bears witness to a vision of the Christian life oriented around the simple but profound message of "faith working by love."

So many dear mentors, colleagues, and friends instilled a great love of the Wesleyan tradition in me. All of them were women and men of deep faith, preachers and singers of love. My middle name—Wesley—is from my maternal grandfather and not directly from John or Charles. But both my father's and mother's families were Methodists to the core. My father was a phenomenal preacher who, like John, proclaimed the faith primarily through that medium. My mother was an amazing musician who, like Charles, sang her faith. I owe so much to my family for the ways in which they formed my spirit.

Among those who taught me to love my tradition, several mentors and colleagues stand out, to whom I owe a similar debt. Ed Senne, a Lutheran, encouraged me to explore my Methodist roots when I was an undergraduate at Valparaiso University. Although ordained in another tradition, Ed was a Methodist at heart, particularly in his work for justice in the world. Frank Baker, my PhD supervisor, and Nellie, his wife, drew me directly into a serious study of John's writings and Charles's hymns. Truth be told, I caught the Wesleyan spirit from them, not my studies. They exemplified humility and hospitality in all they did; they were truly holy. I have always considered Bob Cushman to be my theological mentor. No one knew the full range of Christian doctrinal history as he did. His love of the Wesleys enabled me to locate them in a living stream of vital faith and practice.

S T Kimbrough Jr. personifies the spirit of Charles Wesley. No one I know has written about the hymn writer with greater integrity and appreciation. He instilled in me an even greater love of singing the faith than I had before. Given the fact that I have been a lifelong singer, my mentors in the art of sacred song may have shaped my spirit more than any others. Some were Methodists; some were not. But all of them taught me that our world needs beauty, and music is often the key that opens the door of the heart. I remember and give thanks for Dick and Lorena Campbell, Lamar Runestad, L. L. Fleming, Eldon Balko, Roy Reed, Patrick Matsikenyri, Rodney Wynkoop, and John Sinclair.

Several colleagues in Wesley studies have shaped my own

thinking about John and Charles, particularly with regard to their spirituality. Steve Harper has filled many books of his own with important insights about Wesleyan spirituality. But I am primarily indebted to him for conversations over coffee about our spiritual heritage. Randy Maddox is one of those friends with whom I seldom disagree. His knowledge of the Wesleys is massive, and I have benefited from it time and time again. I have had the amazing opportunity to complete twelve Wesley Pilgrimages as a co-leader with my dear friend Steve Manskar. His passion for discipleship and its goal of perfect love still inspires me and calls me onward and upward. David Lowes Watson wrote the foreword to my very first book on the Wesleys. His view of Wesleyan spirituality as the synthesis of an Anglican holiness of intent and a Puritan interior assurance continues to shape my own vision.

In every book I've published, I've expressed my appreciation to my wife, Janet. With regard to this book, she has something of a special place. Janet is one of the best preachers I have ever heard, and I have a high bar. But she also enjoys singing as much as I do. We have sung together in church choirs for nearly fifty years. Her life is something like a template for this book—the perfect combination of sermon and song. Through the practices of preaching and singing and in myriad other ways, she has taught me how to love more fully.

As you pray these prayers and sing these songs, open your heart to the life-transforming power of love.

Christmas Eve 2023
Paul W. Chilcote

Introduction

A Companion Volume

In my earlier book, *Praying in the Wesleyan Spirit,* I attempted to make John Wesley's sermons more accessible by distilling their essence and translating fifty-two of the "Fifty-three Standard Sermons" into prayers. The way these modernized prayers continue to resonate with contemporary readers has been deeply gratifying. The Charles Wesley hymn excerpts that accompanied those prayers, also translated into modern English, provided an opportunity for readers to sing as they prayed.

This complementary volume, *Transformed by Grace,* replicates the format of my earlier book, offering an additional fifty-two John Wesley sermons translated into prayer with fifty accompanying Charles Wesley hymns. A hymn by Isaac Watts and one of John Wesley's translations of a German hymn are the only exceptions. All the rest belong to the "sweet singer" of Methodism. The readings here cover a wide range of topics related to the spiritual life. Given the fact that many of these sermons come from John Wesley's later period, we can gain some sense of his growing spiritual maturity. I have modernized and encapsulated each sermon (or portions of the sermons) in the form of a brief prayer that can be used devotionally or incorporated into worship. I introduce each prayer with the scripture text John Wesley explores in each sermon. I have changed some of the sermon titles to make them more relevant to our own time. I have intentionally synced each of the selections from Charles's hymns with the biblical texts and the themes of the sermons.

Wesleyan Sermons, Prayers, and Hymns

If John Wesley (1703–1791) were alive today, I would describe him as a Fresh Expressions pioneer. He had an entrepreneurial spirit and the kind of self-discipline to lead a movement of renewal in the church. Methodists are still an important part of the Christian family around the globe. The longevity of this movement testifies to his giftedness in this arena. Preaching quickly became a hallmark of the revival he spearheaded within the Church of England. It was his "field preaching" in April 1739 in Bristol that gave birth to Methodism as a movement. Wesley's heart had been strangely warmed the previous year, but it caught fire when he decided "to submit to be more vile" and take his message to the "highways and byways" in Bristol.

Charles Wesley (1707–1788) sang his faith. In his nearly nine thousand hymns, he developed a lyrical theology just as influential as his elder brother's preaching. It may have even been more significant in the long run. Methodists learned their theology by singing it. The younger Wesley was a great poet, and the central theme of his hymns was the love of God. Many early Methodists testified to the transformative power of singing his hymns. By singing the faith, many found faith. Having found faith, they wanted to sing it all the more.

Most of John Wesley's so-called "standard sermons" (explored in my earlier volume) revolved around the way of salvation. They plumbed the depths of themes like repentance, faith, holiness, and the substance of Jesus' preaching through a detailed analysis of his Sermon on the Mount. They explored the experience of salvation by grace through faith—a cardinal theme of the Protestant tradition. They reminded the church of the centrality of the Beatitudes and the Lord's Prayer. In this new devotional work, I've translated fifty-two more of Wesley's sermons into prayers. They are drawn from the remaining ninety-nine sermons of his collection.[1]

These sermons represent a much wider range of spiritual themes. They include traditional theological topics like the Trinity, creation, the image of God, faith, and perfect love, but many focus on practical matters related to the life of faith. Many of these sermons fall into the broad category of spiritual formation and examine the practical questions of every Christian related to topics like temptation, patience,

1. The definitive edition of John Wesley's extant 151 sermons is collected in the first four volumes of *The Works of John Wesley*, edited by Albert C. Outler (Nashville: Abingdon Press, 1984–87). I used this edition for my process of translating Wesley's sermon texts into the forms of prayer and highly recommend it to any who wish to pursue a fuller study of these sermons.

conscience, simplicity, and zeal. One of John's particular concerns later in life was the danger wealth presented to spiritual growth, and several sermons in this collection address this particular impediment. The community of faith—the church—grounded both Wesley brothers, a foundation they coveted for their followers. So, sermons on community, Christian unity, the need to build one another up, and the importance of Holy Communion feature here.

There are several sermons among these additional fifty-two that many subsequent Methodists wish Wesley had included among the standards. His sermon on "Free Grace," for example, certainly falls into this category. Here Wesley explicates his consistent view of grace as a divine gift in all and for all. "On Working Out Our Own Salvation" is one of his best explanations of the way of salvation and redemption as restoration. Likewise, his sermon "On Perfection" explores his vision of the goal toward which all life in Christ moves—one of his perennial themes. Eucharist featured prominently in the spirituality of both John and Charles. They advocated not only a frequent celebration of the sacrament but "The Duty of Constant Communion." At a time when some of his followers were clamoring for separation from the Church of England, John published "On Schism," an unapologetic defense of unity in the church. Finally, "On Zeal" provides one of Wesley's best blueprints for Christian discipleship.

The Wesleys practiced what they sang and sang what they practiced. Charles put all these themes, topics, and questions into poetic forms. Over the course of more than half a century, the brothers published various collections of *Hymns and Sacred Poems*, primarily the work of Charles, as well as themed hymn books like *Hymns on the Trinity, Hymns on the Nativity,* and *Intercession Hymns.* Of all the collections of hymns John and Charles published, however, no hymn book was of greater importance than the 1780 *Collection of Hymns for the Use of the People Called Methodists.*[2] This collection can be described aptly as the "standard hymns," parallel to John's standard sermons. These hymns functioned as a primer in practical theology and Christian discipleship for the Methodist people.

For Methodists of virtually every stripe, both head and heart are important. And if head and heart are working together as God intends, then hands inevitably get involved as well! What better way for people to encounter this rich treasury of Christian witness than to pray it, sing it, and then translate it into action. The Wesleyan way of living the Christian faith is dynamic and profoundly relational. It is a process of faith working by love leading to holiness of heart and life. Walk with Christ through these prayers, both read and sung, and invite the Holy Spirit to be your companion along the way. God be with you on the journey.

---

2. Most of the hymn excerpts in this book are drawn from this collection, the definitive edition of which is Franz Hildebrandt and Oliver Beckerlegge, eds., *The Works of John Wesley,* vol. 7, *A Collection of Hymns for the Use of the People Called Methodists* (Nashville: Abingdon Press, 1983). Other hymns are drawn from the definitive editions compiled by Randy L. and Aileen Maddox and accessible in The Center for Studies in the Wesleyan Tradition, Duke Divinity School: https://divinity.duke.edu/initiatives/wesleyan-methodist/cswt-cw-published.

Suggestions for Using These Readings

THERE ARE A number ways you can use this resource. Perhaps the most obvious is to center each of the fifty-two weeks of the year on each of the readings. You may want to read the selection on Sunday, at the beginning of the week, or read it daily throughout the course of the week. In this way, you will immerse yourself in the Wesleyan way through the course of a full year. You may actually want to obtain a copy of Wesley's sermons and read them in their entirety in conjunction with these prayers or dip into the larger collections of Charles Wesley's hymns.

Another possibility is to use the prayers at the beginning and ending of each day. If you were to pray selections one and two on the first day, three and four on the second, and so forth through the fifty-two, you would be able to make your way through the entire collection in the course of a month (actually twenty-six days with Sundays left out for other religious practices and corporate worship). The liturgical seasons of Advent and Lent would be particularly appropriate times for this approach.

Yet another option would be to read the prayers and hymns in their entirety, straight through. The advantage of this, of course, is that you obtain the big picture in one sitting. To have a sense of the whole is often very helpful. But since these are prayers, they do call for a more devotional pace of reading. Time for reflection—allowing the prayers and hymns to sink into your spirit—is also important. A day apart or a day-long retreat might provide the opportunity to reflect on these readings in a more leisurely and spiritually uplifting way.

These selections might be put to particularly significant use in corporate contexts, for example, in prayer groups, covenant discipleship groups, Bible studies, class meetings, and Sunday or midweek worship.

In a separate appendix, I have provided a listing of the scriptural texts associated with each prayer/sermon in their canonical order. You may prefer to read through these selections in the order of the texts, giving attention to and time for meditation upon each of the biblical passages. You may also find it helpful to examine the brief text in its larger context in scripture. Note the amazing range and diversity of texts that John Wesley used. There is great breadth and depth here.

Open yourself to the leading of the Spirit. However you choose to use this book, approach the experience prayerfully. Ask God to speak to you through the insights of the Wesleys and their vision of the Christian way. And once you have engaged in prayer using these texts, think about what steps you need to take to put them into action, to live them out in your daily life. It is in this faith working by love that

God's transforming power can be most powerfully experienced in our lives.

Pray, without ceasing pray
(Your Captain gives the word),
His summons cheerfully obey,
And call upon the Lord;
To God your every want
In instant prayer display;
Pray always; pray, and never faint;
Pray, without ceasing pray. (*Collection 259: 4*)

1 ~
The Eternal God

Scripture:

From forever in the past to forever in the future, you are God.

—Psalm 90:2

Prayer:

Eternal God,
As your beloved child, I have no way to comprehend
eternity.
When I look back, I cannot see the beginning;
when I look ahead, I cannot see the end;
But you are Alpha and Omega, the beginning and the
end.
You inhabit eternity.
All I experience and know is time—
a fragment of eternity broken off at both ends.

You waste nothing, and nothing you have created will ever be lost.
You offer me an eternity of blessedness, immersed in your love.
Your holy ones are already praising you in a happy eternity.
They praise you in one still, immovable ocean of love,
and when millions on millions of ages have passed, their eternity has only just begun.
Who would prefer anything to this eternity of praise, joy, and love?
Tragically, many prefer only what they can see here and now.
Faith provides the antidote to this illusion.
Those who put their trust in you, O God of all ages, live in eternity and walk in eternity now.
Gift me with this kind of faith—
Save me from bondage to present things.
Immerse me in the boundless, unfathomable ocean of your love,
which has no bottom and has no shore.
God of all time and space, Alpha and Omega,
How wide your glories shine,
Lord of the universe and mine! Amen.

Hymn:

O God, our help in ages past,
Our hope for years to come,

Our shelter from the stormy blast,
    And our eternal home;

Under the shadow of your throne
    Still may we dwell secure:
Sufficient is your arm alone,
    And our defense is sure.

O God, our help in ages past,
    Our hope for years to come,
Be now our guard while life shall last,
    And our eternal home.

(Collection 39: 1, 2, 7)

2

The Holy Trinity

Scripture:

For there are three that bear record in heaven,
the Father, the Word, and the Holy Ghost:
and these three are one.

—1 John 5:7 (KJV)

Prayer:

Mysterious Three-One God,
We do not love you because we can calculate the math of the Trinity.
No one can, and to rest in a misconceived ability to comprehend you
only demonstrates our lack of true understanding.
Right doctrine is only part of vital religion, and only a minor part at that.
We cannot explain you.
We struggle to find the right words to talk about you.

When our own words fail and explanations evaporate,
we rest in the words of scripture:
"For there are three that bear record in heaven,
the Father, the Word, and the Holy Ghost: and these three are one."
We believe in so many things we cannot comprehend.
You have set us in a universe with 200 billion galaxies.
We can see it and believe in it, but we cannot comprehend it.
We see the sun, we revel in the light, we breathe the air, we feed off the land,
but we hardly understand how all this holds together.
Our souls are the essence of who we are, and they are united to our bodies.
The mystery we are communes with mystery that is you.
You have revealed yourself to us, O mysterious God, and upon this we rely;
we have no need to comprehend in order to believe;
rather, we believe in order to more fully understand.
Thanks be to you, beloved Three-One God,
for your Spirit bears witness with our spirits
that we are your beloved children.
Your Holy Spirit witnesses that the Creator of all things
has embraced each one of us through Jesus, our Lord.
Holy, holy, holy Lord, God of power and might,
heaven and earth are full of your glory. Amen.

Hymn:

Father, Son, and Holy Ghost,
One in Three, and Three in One,
As by the heavenly host
Let your will on earth be done:
Praise by all to you be given,
Glorious Lord of earth and heaven!

Take my soul and body's powers,
Take my memory, mind, and will;
All my goods, and all my hours,
All I know, and all I feel!
All I think, and speak, and do;
Take my heart and make it new!

(Collection 418: 1, 4)

3

God's Love of All Creation

Scripture:

God saw everything he had made: it was supremely good.

—Genesis 1:31

Prayer:

Loving Creator,
You love everything you have made.
You declared everything and everyone good—supremely good.
You created each of us to promote the good of the whole;
to proclaim your goodness through who we are and all we do.
We stand in awe of the diversity that characterizes your creation;

even more, we marvel at the intricate connection among all things.

Earth, water, air, and fire all declare your glory:

You adorned our earthly home with flowers of every color,

shrubs and trees of every kind, fertile plains and glorious mountains.

The great deep, covering our globe, remains shrouded in mystery,

but all life emerges from it, and water sustains all things.

Air fills our lungs and establishes the primary rhythm of life;

we inhale the fresh, the good—we exhale to cleanse.

Through the gift of fire, you keep us warm and provide light in our darkness;

it mesmerizes and plays, strong and pure.

We praise you, loving Creator,

because you created all things good, without exception.

How could it be otherwise?

You have no defect, and your power is the power of love.

Your goodness inclined you to make all things good.

Your creation declares—goodness, beauty, love!

Let all things their Creator praise! Praise the Lord! Amen.

Hymn:

O Praise the Lord! 'tis good to raise,
Your hearts and voices in God's praise;

God's nature and God's works invite
To make this duty our delight.

Sing to the Lord; exalt God high,
Who spreads the clouds around the sky;
There God prepares the fruitful rain,
Nor lets the drops descend in vain.

Each child is lovely in God's sight,
God views all children with delight!
Their hope God sees, and knows their fear,
God looks, and loves God's image there.
(Collection 216: 1, 3, 6, by Isaac Watts)

4 ~
God's Free Gift

Scripture:

The free gift of Christ isn't like Adam's failure.

—Romans 5:15

Prayer:

Wise and Healing God,
Sometimes it's just so hard for me to understand my own brokenness.
If I am honest with myself, pride, selfishness, and hostility
sometimes surface in my feelings and my actions,
driving me away from the goodness and perfect love you intend.
I am a child of Adam—fallen and broken—prone to death, not life.
Why? Why did you create me like this?
Why do I use my freedom to turn away from you?

The simple fact that I'm far from
what you intend me to be
provides an opportunity for Christ to show his
bountiful love to me.
If things were not as they are, I might have loved you as
my Creator,
but I would never have loved you as my dearest Love,
because, in Christ, you gave your life for me!
You overwhelm me; I fall and own that you are God.
What kind of love is this that the only-begotten Son
of God
loves me!
What a grand paradox. You created me in your image.
You gave me understanding and liberty.
You permit me to abuse my freedom; I fall and fall
again.
But through Christ, because of your wisdom, justice,
and mercy,
you offer me an even greater happiness than I ever
could have known.
Fallen, broken, and in desperate need,
you offer me the free gift of your healing love.
I open my broken heart to you, and you fill it with
your love. Amen.

Hymn:

You are good, and good you do,
Your mercies reach to all;
Seekers put their trust in you,
And for your mercy call.

New they every morning are;
As parents, when their children cry,
Never once their pity spare,
And all their needs supply.

Mercy o'er your works presides;
Your providence displayed
Still preserves, and still provides
For all your hands have made;
Keeps, with most distinguished care,
The one who on your love depends,
Watches every numbered hair,
And every step attends.

(Collection 236: 1, 2)

5

The Mission of Christ

Scripture:

God's Son appeared for this purpose: to destroy the works of the devil.

1 John 3:8

Prayer:

Lover of Virtue,
Sometimes I just feel undone.
I do not do the good I want to do and I do what I know to be wrong.
I need your help to discern the difference between good and evil.
Even more important, I need your help to conquer evil and live into the goodness you desire for us all.
I know that you created me in your own image.
You gave me understanding and will and liberty

that I might love, desire, and delight in that which is good.

You also created me for true holiness, that I might enjoy unspeakable happiness,

dwell in you, and have uninterrupted fellowship with you in your goodness.

Because I am like you, O God, I want to be you.

I am not content to be your beloved; I want to be God.

When I feel undone because of my failure,

remind me about the purpose of Christ's mission in the world.

Remind me that Christ came to destroy the power of evil

and to fill me with every good and perfect gift.

The Spirit enables me to cry out, "My Lord and my God,"

and empowers me to live a virtuous life by trusting in him

who loved me and gave himself for me.

By indwelling my heart, Christ effectually destroys the grasp of evil.

You begin the process of restoring your image in me

by striking at the deep root of pride

and then at the persistent root of self-will.

You restore love and joy unspeakable—real substantial happiness. Amen.

Hymn:

Once you did on earth appear,
For humankind t'atone;

Now be manifested here,
And bid our sin be gone!
Come, and by your presence chase
Its nature, with its guilt and power!
Jesu, show your open face,
And sin shall be no more.

You, who did so greatly stoop
To a poor virgin's womb,
Humbly your abode take up;
To me, my Savior, come!
Come, and darkness now destroy,
And let me all your Godhead prove,
Filled with peace, and heavenly joy,
And pure, eternal love.

(Collection 401: 1, 2)

6

Love Is on the Move

Scripture:

The earth will surely be filled with the knowledge of
the Lord,
just as the water covers the sea.

—Isaiah 11:9

Prayer:

God on the move,
We lament the condition of the world in which we live;
darkness, ignorance, and misery seem to rule.
We know that you want love to fill the world,
but where are mercy and love in the face of malice
and brutality?
You intended the church to be a beacon set on a hill;
a community set apart to bear witness to your love.
You intend your people to be ambassadors of
reconciliation,

but where is our witness in the face of our own
animosity and division?
Our hearts break when we see the church erect barriers
to your reign and the establishment of your rule.
If only we were able to fill the earth with a loving
knowledge of you
so that holiness and happiness might cover the earth
and fill every soul!
You could have easily brought in your reign of love through
one unilateral act;
you could have declared, "Let there be love."
But irresistible, coerced love is not love;
your mission of love calls for partnership, not
command.
We pray that your rule will silently flow through us and
among us,
spreading from heart to heart, from home to home,
from town to town, from nation to nation.
We pray that you will use us in renewing the face of the
earth,
that we might bear witness to the eternal reign of mercy,
and that you will establish universal happiness,
causing all to sing:
Blessing and glory and honor and power and might
be to our God forever and always. Amen.

Hymn:

Lord, if you pronounce the word
That forms our souls again,
Love and harmony restored

Throughout our earth shall reign;
When your wondrous love they feel
The human savages are tame;
Ravenous wolves and leopards dwell
And stable with the lamb.

O that now, with pardon blessed,
We each might each embrace!
Quietly together rest,
And feed upon your grace,
Like our sinless parents live!
Great Shepherd, make your goodness known,
All into your fold receive,
And keep us ever one!

(Collection 436: 2, 3)

7 ঌ
New Creation

Scripture:

Look! I'm making all things new.

—Revelation 21:5

Prayer:

God of All Restoration,
When you say, "Look! I'm making all things new,"
we can hardly grasp the full meaning of these words.
We look expectantly for new heavens and a new earth—
a universal restoration, the likes of which we cannot conceive.
The air will be torn no more by hurricanes
or agitated by furious and destructive storms.
All will be light, fair, serene—
a lovely picture of the eternal day.
Fire—that general destroyer of all things—

will destroy and consume no more.
It will be harmless in a new heaven and earth,
the essential component, the energy, of all living things.
Pure, cool, and clean water
will refresh and adorn the earth.
Rivers will gently glide along
for the use and the pleasure of all.
The earth will no longer be frozen by intense cold
or parched with extreme heat.
Rather, everything will be conducive to fruitfulness
and everything produced will benefit everyone.
In the new creation, no creature will kill or hurt or cause pain.
You will wipe away every tear from our eyes and destroy death.
We long for your new creation, for deep, intimate,
an uninterrupted union with you and with all things in you. Amen.

Hymn:

If drawn by your alluring grace
My lack of living faith I feel,
Show me in Christ your smiling face;
What flesh and blood can ne'er reveal,
Your coeternal Son display,
And call my darkness into day.

The gift unspeakable impart:
Command the light of faith to shine,

To shine in my dark, drooping heart,
  And fill me with the life divine;
Now bid the new creation be!
O God, let there be faith in me!
(Collection 142: 2, 3)

8

God's Providential Care

Scripture:

Even the hairs on your head are all counted.

—Luke 12:7

Prayer:

Eternal, All-wise God,
You care for every part of your creation.
Nothing is too small or insignificant according to you;
you desire the happiness of every creature—even me.
You created this whole universe—all that is—out of nothing.
You declared that every distinct part of this universe is good.
When you saw everything in connection, you said it was very good.
You also sustain everything.
You are the preserver as well as the creator of all things.

Christ, the Light, maintains everything.
You see and know everything thoroughly.
You know all the connections, dependencies, and relations.
You see and know my heart; you empathize with every situation I face.
You are infinite in wisdom as well as power.
With your wisdom, you manage all things for the good of all.
Your wisdom and goodness are inseparably united.
Because your loving care—mysterious as it is—extends to everyone,
there can be no distinction between general and particular providence.
Your providential care extends to everyone like beams of light from the sun.
While your providence is a mystery I cannot fully comprehend,
I put my whole trust in you, caring God, because you never fail me.
I give thanks to you because you have protected and delivered me.
I seek to walk humbly with you because you are wise, good, and true.
I seek to walk closely with you because you are the God of love. Amen.

Hymn:

Father of all, whose powerful voice
Called forth this universal frame,

Whose mercies over all rejoice,
    Through endless ages still the same;
You by your word uphold it all;
    Your bounteous love to all is showed;
You hear your every creature's call,
    And fill up every mouth with good.

You, sovereign Lord, let all confess
    That moves in earth, or air, or sky,
Revere your power, your goodness bless,
    Acclaim your providential eye;
All you who owe to God your birth,
    In praise your every hour employ;
Jehovah reigns! Be glad, O earth,
    And shout, ye morning stars, for joy.

(Collection 225: 1, 3)

9

The Wisdom of God

Scripture:

God's riches, wisdom, and knowledge are so deep!

—*Romans 11:33*

Prayer:

Wise and All-knowing God,
All creation bears witness to your wisdom, power, and love.
All things together declare your glory;
you seek the happiness of every living thing.
You display the varieties of your wisdom through the church.
In the fullness of time, you sent Jesus to lay the foundation;
those who followed him lived in peace, broke bread together, and prayed.
While the form of religion remained, however, the power of true love declined.

You raised up prophets to call us back to your purposes;
you sowed seeds of hope through those beckoned by your love.
You still renew the church through those you call to be gospel-bearers.
Like them, you call us to be simple of heart and devoted to you;
you make us zealous for good works, desiring only the whole image of Christ.
Nothing pulls us away from our mission more than our affluence.
Teach us again to earn all we can and save all we can;
then set our hearts free to give all we can.
Whenever your beloved family falters, you raise up a new generation.
Fill us with your Spirit and draw us together into the new life you offer;
may we be your faithful people who bear witness to your wisdom and love.
May we be a chosen generation that proclaims the glory of your love.
Reshape us into a royal priesthood, a holy nation;
the people you embrace as your own.
May we speak of the wonderful acts of the One
who called us out of darkness into such amazing light,
beloved, wise, good God. Amen.

Hymn:

You, the great eternal Lord,
  Are high above our thought!
Worthy to be feared, adored
  By those your hands have wrought;
None can with yourself compare,
Your glory fills both earth and sky,
We and all your creatures are
  As nothing in your eye.

You, O God, are wise alone,
  Your counsel does excel;
Wonderful your works we own,
  Your ways unsearchable,
Who can sound the mystery,
Your judgments' deep abyss explain—
Give us hearts and eyes to see
  The wonder of your reign.

(Collection 235: 1, 3)

10 ~
The Community of Faith

Scripture:

I encourage you to live as people worthy of the call you received from God. Conduct yourselves with all humility, gentleness, and patience. Accept each other with love, and make an effort to preserve the unity of the Spirit with the peace that ties you together. You are one body and one spirit, just as God also called you in one hope. There is one Lord, one faith, one baptism, and one God and Father of all, who is over all, through all, and in all.

—Ephesians 4:1-6

Prayer:

Gracious God,
We know that whenever two or three of us
gather in the name of Jesus, he is with us.
The word "church" does not mean a building or a structure;

the church is a community, gathered as one in Christ.
We give you thanks, O God, because
one Spirit breathes life into our family,
one Lord rules over us all,
one faith—your free gift—shapes our lives,
one baptism links us to one another forever,
and you—our one God and parent—dwell in our hearts.
We give you thanks, O God, for uniting all the people in the universe
whom you have called out of the world and into this family of love.
We pray that we will be people worthy of the call we received from you.
Help us to be humble—to assume the posture of Christ our Lord.
Help us to be meek—to obey the teachings of our Master.
Help us to be long-suffering—to embrace the patience we see in Jesus.
Help us to carry one another's burdens—to fulfill the law of love.
Enable us, we pray, to preserve the unity of the Spirit
with the peace that ties us all together.
You intend all of us to be holy as you are holy.
Help us, then, to walk in the light as you are in the light.
Shine through us so that all will be able to see the good things you do
and praise your blessed name forever. Amen.

Hymn:

Father, Son, and Spirit, hear
Faith's effectual, fervent prayer!
Hear, and our petitions seal;
Let us now the answer feel.

Build us in one body up,
Called in one high calling's hope.
One the Spirit whom we claim,
One the pure, baptismal flame;

One the faith and common Lord,
One the Father lives adored,
Over, through, and in us all,
God incomprehensible.

(Collection 501: 1, 3, 4)

11
Lamenting Christian Division

Scripture:

So that there won't be division in the body.

—1 Corinthians 12:25

Prayer:

God of Peace,
We lament division within the life of the church.
It destroys our family and compromises our mission in the world.
Schism is not separation from but division in the church.
We lament the way in which we divide into rival groups
instead of seeking the same mind and the same purpose.
We lament the way in which opinions about doctrine
divide us into competing parties—a greater heresy.
We lament the way in which our differences
lead us to abandon genuine care for one another.

Whenever we separate ourselves from other Christians,
we break the law of love.
The pretenses for division may be innumerable,
but lack of love is always the real cause.
Forgive us, Lord Jesus,
because you have commanded
that we love each other just as you have loved us.
Forgive us, Lord Jesus,
because our failure to love opens the door
to anger, resentment, bitterness, and malice.
Forgive us, Lord Jesus,
because our divisions and schisms in the church
destroy our witness to the power of love to heal and unite.
Whoever loves dispute does not love you!
So help us to follow your word:
Pursue the goal of peace with everyone.
Shun evil and do good; overcome evil with good.
Amen.

Hymn:

Sweetly may we all agree,
Touched with softest sympathy;
Kindly for each other care,
Every member feel its share.

Many are we now, and one,
We who Jesus have put on;
There is neither bond nor free,
Male nor female, Lord, in thee!

Love, like death, hath all destroyed,
Rendered our distinctions void!
Names, and sects, and parties fall,
You, O Christ, are all in all!

(Collection 504: 7, 9, 10)

12 ~
Christian Maturity

Scripture:

So let's press on to maturity.

—Hebrews 6:1

Prayer:

God of Lofty Ideals,
The idea of perfection is out of favor these days.
Many people mistake it for perfectionism—a pathology.
But perfection, or maturity, is a noble ideal to pursue.
When I view perfection in terms of Christian maturity—
the fullest possible growth in love—
why would I not want to strive for this?
Here is the perfection—the maturity—I long for, O God:
to love you with my whole heart;
to have the mind that was in Christ;
to exhibit the fruit of the Spirit—love, joy, peace, patience,

kindness, goodness, faithfulness, gentleness, and
self-control;
to have the loving image of Christ renewed in my
very being;
to grow into the fullest possible holiness of heart and
life.
God of peace, sanctify me wholly.
May every part of who I am—spirit, soul, and body—
be kept blameless at the coming of our Lord Jesus Christ.
I know that you long for me to be unspeakably holy and
happy.
You don't want love to visit me like a transient guest;
you want love to be the ruling character of my life.
Remove every impediment, every barrier,
to your loving work in my life!
Help me to throw off any extra baggage,
get rid of the sin that trips me up,
and fix my eyes on Jesus,
the pioneer and perfector of
faith that works by love. Amen.

Hymn:

O for a heart to praise my God,
A heart from sin set free!
A heart that always feels thy blood,
So freely spilt for me!

A heart in every thought renewed,
And full of love divine,

Perfect, and right, and pure, and good—
    A copy, Lord, of thine!

Thy nature, gracious Lord, impart;
    Come quickly from above;
Write thy new name upon my heart,
    Thy new, best name of Love!
                (Collection 334: 1, 4, 8)

13
Spiritual Worship

Scripture:

This is the true God and eternal life.

—1 John 5:20

Prayer:

Glorious yet Intimate God,
Spiritual worship happens when I am in
happy and holy communion with you—
the Father, Son, and Holy Spirit.
I know that I am your child,
by the witness and the fruit of your Spirit.
You are the true God,
the sole Creator of all things.
You are the true God,
the gracious Sustainer of all things.
You are the true God,
the patient Preserver of all connected things.

You are the true God,
  the purposeful Author of all motion in the universe.
You are the true God,
  the willing Redeemer of all your children.
You are the true God,
  the just Governor of your universal realm.
You are the true God,
  the happy End of all things—
    the goal toward which all things move.
Jesus Christ, you are my eternal life,
  the Author of salvation to whom I entrust my life;
  the Vine in which I dwell and grow in love;
  the Love that has taken full possession of my heart,
    calming my restlessness and enabling me
    to worship you in spirit and in truth. Amen.

Hymn:

Thou hidden love of God, whose height,
  Whose depth unfathomed no one knows;
I see from far thy beauteous light,
  Inly I sigh for thy repose;
My heart is pained, nor can it be
At rest, till it finds rest in thee.

Is there a thing beneath the sun
  That strives with thee my heart to share?
Ah! tear it thence, and reign alone,
  The Lord of every motion there!
Then shall my heart from earth be free,
When it hath found repose in thee.

(Collection 335: 1, 4)

14

On Temptation

Scripture:

> No temptation has seized you that isn't common for people. But God is faithful. He won't allow you to be tempted beyond your abilities. Instead, with the temptation, God will also supply a way out so that you will be able to endure it.
>
> —*1 Corinthians 10:13*

Prayer:

Merciful God,
The fact that I can so easily fall off your path of love
worries me and convicts me about the necessity of
vigilance.
Ingratitude and disobedience steal their way into my
heart;
temptations follow me wherever I go, and I so easily
succumb.

I experience the same kinds of temptations common to us all.
My body sometimes gets in my way;
it makes me susceptible to all kinds of temptations.
My soul gets weighed down by the burdens of life;
even though I am close to you, I am still in danger.
The world around me pulls me in so many directions;
I feel seduced to move away from your will and way.
Even those who love you, O God, are sometimes sources of temptation;
even they can induce me to think and act in harmful ways.

It is such a comfort to know you are with me, protecting me.
When I am tempted, you offer me an escape, an outlet;
your faithfulness, as well as your mercy, surrounds me.
When I am tempted, you deliver me out of temptation;
your intervention removes the obstacle from my path.

Whenever I think I can stand,
remind me that I need to watch out or else I might fall.
Help me to remember who I am and to whom I belong.
Help me to rely on your strength when I am weak.
Help me to rest in your mercy, faithfulness, and power. Amen.

Hymn:

Jesus, my strength and hope,
On you I cast my care,
With humble confidence look up,
And know you hear my prayer.
Give me on you to wait,
Till I can all things do,
On you almighty to create,
Almighty to renew.

I want a godly fear,
A quick-discerning eye,
That looks to you when sin is near
And sees the tempter fly;
A spirit still prepared
And armed with jealous care,
Forever standing on its guard,
And watching unto prayer.

(Collection 292: 1, 3)

15 ~
On Patience

Scripture:

Let this endurance complete its work so that you may be fully mature, complete, and lacking in nothing.

—James 1:4

Prayer:

Lord,
I want to be patient in my heart—
  I want a gracious disposition deep down within,
    cultivated by the continual work of the Holy Spirit.
I want to be patient in my life—
  I want a genuine sense of peace in my heart,
    neither fretful nor dejected, but content in all things.
Grant to me this gift of patience:
    a sweet tranquility of mind,
    a serenity of spirit,

an elevated sense of joy,
an even temper of quiet expectation,
a hope for the best in the midst of suffering,
a habitual love of Christ and trust in you.
Grant to me the fruits of patience:
the perfect love of you,
the love of every soul,
the mind that was in Christ,
the renewal of Christ's image in my life,
the offering of my whole self, body, and spirit to you—
continual love and joy flooding my soul.
Lord, I want to be patient in my heart and in my life. Amen.

Hymn:

I want a true regard,
A single, steady aim,
Unmoved by threatening or reward,
To you and your great name;
A jealous, just concern
For your immortal praise;
A pure desire that all may learn
And glorify your name.

I rest upon your Word,
The promise is for me;
My succor, and salvation, Lord,
Shall surely set me free.
But let me still abide,

Nor from my hope remove,
Till you my patient spirit guide
Into your perfect love.
(Collection 292: 5, 6)

16
The Important Question

Scripture:

Why would people gain the whole world but lose their lives?

—Matthew 16:26

Prayer:

Guardian of Our Souls,
We fall prey so easily to the temptations of the world.
Why would we want to gain the whole world but lose our lives?
Forgive us for seeking those things that can never really satisfy us:
for gratifying ourselves in a life of worldly pleasures;
for lusting after the best, grandest, and newest things;
for craving status, glory, and fame for ourselves;
for coveting the praise and applause of the crowd.
Convict us about what it means if we lose our souls:

sacrificing the comfort, joy, and peace of true religion;
abandoning the memories of a life well-lived;
relinquishing the delights of paradise, the garden of God;
never hearing those words,
"Well done. You are a good and faithful servant."
Forgive us for thinking a spiritual life means a life of misery.
True religion is neither more nor less than love:
love ruling the whole life,
animating our character,
directing our thoughts,
guiding our words and actions.
May our communion with you fill us with joy unspeakable.
May our connection with others help us love more freely.
Fill our imaginations with the vision of a life
lost in wonder, love, and praise. Amen.

Hymn:

Whom have we on earth below?
You, and only you we know:
Whom have we in heaven but you?
You are all in all and true.

Love alone we elevate,
Grace and peace we celebrate;
Earthly treasures we despise,
Love is all our paradise.

Nothing else can we require,
Love fills up our whole desire:
All your other gifts remove;
Still you give us all in love.

(Collection 422: 4, 6, 7)

17 ~

On Working Out Our Own Salvation

Scripture:

Carry out your own salvation with fear and trembling. God is the one who enables you both to want and to actually live out his good purposes.

—Philippians 2:12-13

Prayer:

Prevenient God,
Every day, we navigate a great paradox.
We must hold together two competing ideas about life:
that you are the one at work within us;
that you call us to work out our own salvation.
All day long, you are at work for good in the world.
That includes each of us—all we have and are,

and the life of your great community of love—the church.
Because your work is prevenient—coming before everything else—this removes all claims to our own merit
and gives you the whole glory for your own work.
You want only the very best for each of us—
you breathe every good desire into us
and bring it to fruition in your good time.
If we know and feel that you initiate every impulse for good,
and that you empower us to work toward love's goals,
then how we can brag about anything but you?
In carrying out our own salvation, then, we celebrate
our first wish to please you,
our deeper self-understanding,
our trust and confidence in you,
our growth in love toward you and others.
Because you put your love to work in us,
we want to work with you toward a fuller love.
Your goal is for love to mature in each of us—
to be fully grown, fully human,
measured by the standard of the fullness of Christ.
Amen.

Hymn:

To you, O God, our souls we lift,
Our souls on you depend,
Convinced that every perfect gift
Will from your heart descend.

Mercy and grace are yours alone,
  And power and wisdom too;
Without the Spirit of your Son
  We nothing good can do.

From you, through Jesus, we receive
  The power on you to call,
In whom we are, and move, and live—
  Our God is all in all.

(Collection 423: 1, 2, 6)

18

The Danger of Riches

Scripture:

But people who are trying to get rich fall into temptation. They are trapped by many stupid and harmful passions that plunge people into ruin and destruction.

—*1 Timothy 6:9*

Prayer:

God of the Poor,
So many things in life draw me away from you.
But nothing ensnares me more than wealth.
When I think about most of the people in the world,
I am already rich beyond imagination.
Regardless, I confess that I want more—I want more than I need—
I am captured by the desire for more things, meaningless things.

I accumulate so many things I simply do not need;
I delight in them and really believe they will bring me happiness.
Riches gratify my imagination:
They make me long for whatever I see—sensual indulgence.
They accentuate my need for applause from others.
They make me lazy in life—morally irresponsible.
They accelerate the dispositions of greed and envy.
Save me, O God, from the pride that comes with riches—
make me humble of heart.
Save me, O God, from the haughty spirit that accompanies wealth—
make me meek and lowly of spirit.
Save me, O God, from the arrogance aligned with affluence—
make me patient and content in all things.
Save me, O God, from a sense of superiority to others—
make me zealous for works of mercy and piety.
Write this upon my heart:
"It will be very hard for a rich person to enter the kingdom of heaven.
In fact, it's easier for a camel to squeeze through the eye of a needle than for a rich person to enter God's kingdom." Amen.

Hymn:

Nothing on earth I call my own;
A stranger, to the world unknown,
I all their goods despise;

I trample on their whole delight,
And seek a country out of sight,
    A country in the skies.

There is my house and portion fair,
My treasure and my heart is there,
    And my abiding home;
For me my elder brethren stay,
And angels beckon me away,
    And Jesus bids me come!

(Collection 66: 6, 8)

19

The Simple Life

Scripture:

> Don't try to make yourselves beautiful on the outside, with stylish hair or by wearing gold jewelry or fine clothes. Instead, make yourselves beautiful on the inside, in your hearts, with the enduring quality of a gentle, peaceful spirit. This type of beauty is very precious in God's eyes.
>
> —*1 Peter 3:3-4*

Prayer:

Patient God,
I know that transformation comes through conformity to Christ.
Nevertheless, I find myself perennially attracted to worldly things.
I don't want to appear out of step with those around me;

I want to be just like everyone else—just more in
vogue.
Instead of focusing my attention on what is good,
acceptable, and perfect in your eyes,
I am more concerned about trifles.
I can be so superficial;
silly concerns like what I wear consume my thoughts.
I am tempted to ask, What does this even matter?
What possible harm could there be in what I put on?
Is it not my right to do as I please?
But the Spirit stops me in my tracks!
Those fine clothes breed vanity.
Those diamonds and gold jewelry engender pride.
That appetite to outdo others leads to envy.
Your Spirit even cuts me to the quick!
The more I accumulate costly clothing,
the less I have to clothe those who have nothing,
the less I have to feed the hungry and lodge the
stranger,
the less I have to relieve the sick, imprisoned, and
distressed.
You call me, O God, to a simple life—
to live simply that others may simply live.
Guard me, then, from trying to make myself beautiful
on the outside.
Make me beautiful on the inside, in my heart,
with the enduring quality of a gentle, peaceful spirit.
I know that this beauty is much more precious in your
sight. Amen.

Hymn:

Send down your likeness from above,
   And let this my adorning be;
Clothe me with wisdom, patience, love,
   With lowliness and purity,
Than gold and pearls more precious far,
And brighter than the morning star.

Lord, arm me with your Spirit's might,
   Since I am called by your great name;
In you let all my thoughts unite,
   Of all my works be you the aim;
Your love attend me all my days,
And my sole business be your praise.

(Collection 419: 5, 6)

20

The More Excellent Way

Scripture:

Use your ambition to try to get the greater gifts.
And I'm going to show you an even better way.
—*1 Corinthians 12:31*

Prayer:

Great Companion,
We know that the life of faith is more than belief in certain things;
it is a journey in which you accompany us as our guide and friend.
The way of love, of loving all people for your sake,
the life of humble, gentle, patient love,
is the more excellent way.
You give all of us gifts to use in this journey with Jesus.
But without love, all these gifts—
all knowledge about you and your way,

all faith, even faith to remove mountains,
all works, all our efforts to promote goodness,
all our suffering on your behalf—
are of no more value in your sight
than sounding brass or rumbling cymbals.
All we know, believe, do, and suffer
means nothing apart from love.
Your more excellent way of love
touches every practical aspect of our lives:
Help us moderate our sleep so as to be more awake to you.
Help us pray so as to open our hearts to your world.
Help us work so as to become beacons of hope to others.
Help us nourish our bodies so as to gain strength to serve.
Help us regulate our conversation so as to communicate your love.
Help us use our resources to elevate the poor and neglected.
From this point on, we will give you all our goods and all our hearts in the service of the more excellent way of love. Amen.

Hymn:

Let us join ('tis God commands)
Let us join our hearts and hands;
Help to gain our calling's hope,
Build we each the other up.

God a blessing shall dispense,
God shall crown this ordinance,
Meet in God's appointed ways,
Nourish us with social grace.

Let us as God's children love,
Faithfully God's gifts improve,
Carry on the earnest strife,
Walk in holiness of life.

(Collection 507: 1, 2a)

21 ❧
Authenticity

Scripture:

Here is a genuine Israelite in whom there is no deceit.

—John 1:47

Prayer:

God of Truth and Love,
If I am to live the way of Christ—the authentic human life—
I must hold truth and love together.
If I am to be true to you and authentic in my love,
I must give you my whole heart.
I give you my heart whenever I seek you fully
and find genuine happiness in you.
If I am to be true to you and authentic in my love,
I must always speak the truth from my heart.
In an age characterized by duplicity,
help me always to be transparent and authentic.

If I am to be true to you and authentic in my love,
  I must be sincere in all my thoughts and actions.
    Despite the cunning and deceit around me,
      help me to demonstrate wisdom and discretion.
If I am to be true to you and authentic in my love,
  I must be simple in heart and spirit.
    Displace my self-absorption;
      help me to be plain and artless in my life.
Fill me with real, genuine, solid virtue;
  not truth alone, nor conformity to truth,
    but truth united with love,
      the essence of all virtue or holiness.
Let humble, gentle, patient love
  be fixed in me on a proper foundation,
    my love of you springing from my faith—
      faith working by love. Amen.

Hymn:

Happy are those who find the grace,
The blessing of God's chosen race,
The wisdom coming from above,
The faith that sweetly works by love.

Happy beyond description they
Who know the price the Lord did pay,
The gift unspeakable t'obtain,
And heavenly understanding gain.

To purest joys they all invite,
In justice, truth, and love delight;
Their ways are ways of righteousness,
That guide all in the paths of peace.
(Collection 14: 1, 2, 5)

22

Humble Love

Scripture:

If I speak in tongues of human beings and of angels but I don't have love, I'm a clanging gong or a clashing cymbal. If I have the gift of prophecy and I know all the mysteries and everything else, and if I have such complete faith that I can move mountains but I don't have love, I'm nothing. If I give away everything that I have and hand over my own body to feel good about what I've done but I don't have love, I receive no benefit whatsoever.

—*1 Corinthians 13:1-3*

Prayer:

Love Incarnate,
You reveal that humble love is the essence of all true religion.
All that is true, all that is holy, all that is just,

all that is pure, all that is lovely,
and all that is worthy of praise,
is subsumed under the simple words—humble love.
To love as you love entails loving our neighbor.
It means assuming the posture of humility.
Guard me against becoming all puffed up.
It means responding to others with gentleness.
Guard me against becoming easily provoked.
It means enduring injuries with patience and kindness.
Guard me against becoming harsh and vindictive.
I may be able to speak persuasively from the heart,
but eloquence without love means nothing.
I may know a lot about you, your will, and your way,
but knowledge without love means nothing.
I may have extraordinary faith,
but spiritual maturity without love means nothing.
I may give away everything to help others,
but sacrifice without love means nothing.
I may endure persecution for your sake,
but suffering without love means nothing.
In addition to all I speak, know, believe, do, or suffer,
enable me to hold fast to the one thing I really need—
the humble love of Christ. Amen.

Hymn:

The depth of all-redeeming love
What angel-tongue can tell?
O may I to the utmost prove
The gift unspeakable!

Come quickly, gracious Lord, and take
  Possession of your own!
My longing heart vouchsafe to make
  Your everlasting throne!

Assert your claim, maintain your right,
  Come quickly from above;
And sink me to perfection's height,
  The depth of humble love.

(Collection 207: 6, 8, 9)

23 ∾
On Zeal

Scripture:

> But it is good to be zealously affected always in a good thing.
>
> —*Galatians 4:18 (KJV)*

Prayer:

God of Fervent Love,
There is so much religious zeal in the world today.
  So much of it alienates people and shatters peace.
But true Christian zeal is about loving you fervently
  and loving our neighbors as passionately as we love
    ourselves.
True Christian zeal is fervent love,
  love that shapes humility, meekness, and patience,
    in the deepest part of my inmost being.
Implant your love on the throne of my soul.
Establish gentleness, faithfulness, and peace—

everything comprising the mind of Christ—
in a circle near the throne.
Institute the works of mercy—
the practices of compassion and justice—
in an exterior circle to benefit others.
Expand my love through works of piety—
the practices of devotion and worship—
in yet another circle of grace in my life.
Finally, unite me together with others in your church,
that others might effectually provoke me
to love and good works.
In all this, I press on for the prize of your
upward call in Christ Jesus. Amen.

Hymn:

Jesus, I fain would find
Your zeal for God in me,
Your pity for all humankind,
Your burning charity.

In me your Spirit dwell!
In me your mercies move!
So shall the fervor of my zeal
Be the pure flame of love.
(Collection 291: 1, 2)

24

Self-Care

Scripture:

Redeeming the time.

—Ephesians 5:16 (KJV)

Prayer:

God of Health and Wholeness,
You are not only concerned about our spiritual welfare.
You care about our physical and emotional needs as well.
You want us to be healthy in every respect.
What we eat, when we rest, and how we exercise—
our self-care—everything from sleep to work
interests you as much as our life of prayer.
First and foremost, convince us that all these things matter.
Teach us the connection of the physical to the spiritual.
Teach us to depend on you for strength
as we work on our physical and emotional health,

rather than trying to do everything ourselves.
Teach us to pray for your power within us,
to embrace a disciplined life in faith,
for your strength is perfected in our weakness.
Teach us to focus our attention on realistic goals,
to be diligent and disciplined
about the means that facilitate good health.
Teach us to be steady and persevering,
to rally when we falter or fail,
and to press on through challenges that arise.
Teach us to view our physical and emotional health
in the same way we view your call
to holiness of heart and life.
We seek to be not almost, but altogether Christians,
to finish our course with joy—
to be happy about who we are: whole and holy.
Amen.

Hymn:

Give me the faith which can remove,
And sink the mountain to a plain!
Give me the child-like, praying love,
Which longs to build your house again;
Your love, let it my heart o'erpower,
And all my simple soul devour.

I would the precious time redeem,
And longer live for this alone,
To spend and to be spent for them
Who have not yet my Savior known;

Fully on these my mission prove,
And only breathe, to breathe your love.
(Collection 421: 1, 3)

25

Family Religion

Scripture:

But my family and I will serve the Lord.

—Joshua 24:15

Prayer:

God from whom every family takes its name,
You have placed us in families—
all shapes and sizes of families—
so that we might learn how to love.
In our families we learn what it means to serve you:
to put our whole trust in Christ,
to love you with our whole heart,
to love others as we love ourselves,
to obey you,
to walk in your ways,
to do your will from our hearts.
Thank you for our families:

for spouses and partners,
for adopted and biological children,
for grandparents and grandchildren,
for all those to whom we provide hospitality.
Thank you for the ways you nurture us in our families:
surrounding us with love,
guarding us from evil,
guiding us in the way of truth,
instructing us with patience,
enlightening us with your wisdom.
We worship you in spirit and in truth
because of the love, which from our birth,
over and around us lies. Amen.

Hymn:

I and my house will serve the Lord.
But first, obedient to God's word
I must myself appear;
By actions, words, and tempers show
That I my heavenly Master know,
And serve with heart sincere.

Lord, if you did the wish infuse,
A vessel fitted for your use
Into your hands receive;
Work in me both to will and do,
And show them how believers true
And real Christians live.

(Collection 460: 1, 4)

26 ~

Spiritual Formation

Scripture:

Train children in the way they should go;
when they grow old, they won't depart from it.

—*Proverbs 22:6*

Prayer:

Guiding Spirit,
We want to be shaped by your creative hand.
Mold us into the people you would have us to be.
We are so deeply aware of the flaws in our character.
Do for us what we cannot do for ourselves.
Plant within us the desire to conform to Christ;
form our spirits anew as we model our lives after his.
When we permit our own wills to rule our thoughts and actions,
help us to submit to your control and direction.

When pride leads us to think more highly of ourselves than we should,
help us to cry out: "Not to us, Lord, but to you be all glory."
When our love of the world pulls our attention away from your way,
help us know, love, and serve you above all things.
When we nurture anger in the citadel of our hearts,
help us to cultivate love and a spirit of reconciliation.
When our preference for darkness leads us to seize upon what's false,
help us to embrace truth, sincerity, and simplicity.
When our indifference to injustice blinds us to others' pain,
help us to sow seeds of justice, peace, and hope.
Reform our spirits so that we long to stay in love,
thereby remaining in you and you in us.
Reshape us into people who follow the example of Christ,
who loved us and gave himself for us. Amen.

Hymn:

Come, Father, Son, and Holy Ghost,
To whom we for ourselves now cry!
The good desired and wanted most
Out of your richest grace supply—
The sacred discipline be given
To train and bring us up for heaven.

Unite the pair so long disjoined,
Knowledge and vital piety:
Learning and holiness combined,

And truth and love, let people see;
For shaped by love, our hearts we give,
Yours, wholly yours, we die and live.

(Collection 461: 1, 5)

27 ঌ
Compassion in Action

Scripture:

I was sick and you took care of me.

—Matthew 25:36

Prayer:

Compassionate God,
It is easy for me to think about my spirituality
in terms of the works of piety—
prayer, scripture, fellowship, and Eucharist.
But if I fixate on these spiritual disciplines,
as if they were the only means of grace,
I easily neglect other life-shaping practices.
You shape love in my heart and life
through exterior works of mercy
that are just as important to my spiritual growth.
Acts of compassion and justice
conform my heart and life

to the mind and way of Christ.
So you call me to a balanced spirituality
in which works of piety and mercy work together
to produce a genuinely Christlike spirit.
As one of your beloved children, I am called to
feed the hungry,
provide water to those who thirst,
offer hospitality to strangers,
clothe those who have little to wear,
visit the sick,
and care for those in prison.
Whenever I do these things for the least among us,
I do them all for you, and you flood my heart with love.
Amen.

Hymn:

Come, let us arise,
And press to the skies;
The summons obey,
My friends, my beloved, and hasten away!
The Master of all
For our service doth call,
And deigns to approve
With smiles of acceptance our labor of love.

Then let us attend
Our heavenly friend,
In his members distressed,
With want, or affliction, or sickness oppressed;
The prisoner relieve,

The stranger receive,
Supply all their wants,
And spend and be spent in assisting God's saints.

(Collection 482: 1, 3)

28 ~

The Christlike Servant

Scripture:

Come, you who will receive good things from my Father. Inherit the kingdom that was prepared for you before the world began.

—Matthew 25:34

Prayer:

God of Active Love,
There is no debate in my mind about good works.
  I am saved by grace through faith,
    but you call me to an active faith that works by love.
Elevating the centrality of faith in salvation
  should never lead to the devaluation of good works—
    faith without works is dead.
Good works that flow from a Christlike spirit
  are the perfection of religion:
    they are the highest part of the spiritual building,
    constructed on the foundation of Christ.

I want to be a miracle of your mercy:
I want to restore health to the broken.
I want to offer helpless children hope.
I want to provide for those who have nothing.
I want to listen to those who have no one.
I want to support the weak and lonely.
I want to guide the fallen into your loving embrace.
I want to elevate the least and last to places of honor.
I want to direct the lost to their proper home.
I want to shine light into the darkness of the world.
Give me courage and strength by your grace
to translate my faith into active love for others.
Shape me into a Christlike servant,
and enlarge my heart to take in the world. Amen.

Hymn:

Affliction, poverty, disease,
Drew out her soul in soft distress,
The wretched to relieve:
In all the works of love employed,
Her sympathizing soul enjoyed
The blessedness to give.

A nursing-mother to the poor,
For them she husbanded her store,
Her life, her all, bestowed:
For them she labored day and night,
Compassion was her whole delight,
In copying after God.

(Funeral Hymns 32: 2, 3)

29
Building Each Other Up

Scripture:

Each of us should please our neighbors for their good in order to build them up.

—Romans 15:2

Prayer:

O God,
Instead of tearing one another down,
we need to find ways to build one another up.
We can be so destructive in our relationships,
so help us to encourage and honor one another.
Guard us
from cruelty, malice, envy, hatred, and revenge;
from pride, haughtiness of spirit, and arrogance;
from overbearing and mercurial behavior;
from dishonesty and dissimulation;
from guile, subtlety, and deception.

May there be no hint of fraud within us;
rather, cultivate a spirit of authenticity deep in our souls.
Shape in us a Christlike spirit:
Let love not visit us as a transient guest,
but be the constant ruling quality of our lives.
Let humility shine through all our words and actions,
so that others might always feel honored and valued.
Let us work and pray to be meek and lowly of heart,
so that others might experience gentleness through us.
Let us offer courtesy to everyone, high or low, rich or poor,
so that others might feel they are true brothers and sisters.
Let us declare the love we really feel for others,
so that all of us might be drawn more fully into your love.
As we seek to build one another up,
may all our actions be rooted in that unbounded love. Amen.

Hymn:

All praise to our redeeming Lord,
Who joins us by his grace,
And bids us, each to each restored,
Together seek his face.

He bids us build each other up,
And gathered into one;

To our high calling's glorious hope
    We hand in hand go on.

We all partake the joy of one,
    The common peace we feel,
A peace to sensual minds unknown,
    A joy unspeakable.
        (Redemption Hymns 32: 1, 3a)

30 ~
Constant Communion

Scripture:

Do this in remembrance of me.

—Luke 22:19

Prayer:

Gracious God,
You invite us to share in Holy Communion
as a means of grace
in which we experience your love.
You have promised to meet us at the table,
so why would we not want to meet you there
at every possible opportunity?
Christ not only commanded us to share this meal,
saying, "Do this in remembrance of me,"
but offers us untold benefits through it.
None of us is worthy to share in this Holy Mystery;

being unworthy is the primary criterion for our invitation;
Jesus joins the hungry and offers his gift of grace to us all.
We need not be concerned about our preparation
because you are always ready and willing
to be with us in whatever state we are.
We need not fear being with you at this meal too often,
because we are always spiritually hungry,
and your desire for us to grow in love never ends.
Even when we feel nothing as we gather around your table,
you are at work within us;
we don't always experience your good gifts immediately.
You long to feed us, both physically and spiritually,
because you love us so deeply and care for us so fully.
Meet us, gracious God, at your table and fill us with love. Amen.

Hymn:

Come, sinners, to the gospel feast,
Let every soul be Jesu's guest,
Ye need not one be left behind,
For God hath bid all humankind.

Sent by my Lord, on you I call,
The invitation is to all:
Come all the world; Come, sinner, thou!
All things in Christ are ready now.

Come, all ye souls by sin oppressed,
Ye restless wanderers after rest;
Ye poor, and maimed, and halt, and blind,
In Christ a hearty welcome find.

(Collection 2: 1, 2, 3)

31 ~

A Good Conscience

Scripture:

> This is why we are confident, and our conscience confirms this.
>
> *—2 Corinthians 1:12*

Prayer:

God of Light,
My conscience is like an internal guidance system—
an interior knowledge of my words and actions,
a sense about their goodness or badness,
an immediate knowledge about the quality of my life.
You give this light to everyone coming into the world;
a good conscience is a gift from you that both convicts and guides.
Your Spirit provides an inward check,
an uneasy feeling about what I say and what I do

whenever I walk contrary to your way and will.

A good conscience has a three-fold function:

it witnesses or testifies to what I have done;

it judges whether my thoughts, words, or actions are godly;

it executes sentence on every evil act by grieving my heart.

My conscience is a spiritual sense that approves goodness and disapproves cruelty in all its ugly forms.

Thank you, God, for creating within me a soul sense

to measure the quality of my thoughts, words, and actions;

to discern the difference between right and wrong;

to rule my spirit and thereby direct my path.

Cultivate in me a tender conscience—a godly principle within—a spirit of calm and peace that nurtures my soul.

The only way for me to preserve my conscience is to obey it; every act of obedience gives me sharper and stronger sight.

Help me to listen to my conscience—the witness of love in my soul—and steadily follow it into your marvelous light. Amen.

Hymn:

I want a principle within
Of jealous, godly fear,
A sensibility of sin,
A pain to feel it near.

That I from you no more may part,
    No more your goodness grieve,
The filial awe, the fleshly heart,
    The tender conscience give.

Quick as the apple of an eye,
    O God, my conscience make;
Awake my soul, when sin is nigh,
    And keep it still awake.
(Collection 299: 1, 2, 3)

32 ~

On Faith

Scripture:

It's impossible to please God without faith.

—Hebrews 11:6

Prayer:

Author of Faith,
I know that faith is the reality of what I hope for,
the proof of what I don't see;
faith means putting my trust in you fully.
But my faith in you is more than trust;
it is an inner conviction about your love,
so powerfully demonstrated to me by Christ.
I pray for those who seem to have little or no faith at all;
they live in a material world without any concern for you.
I pray for those who believe merely that you exist;
they live as if you are detached and distant—uncaring.

I pray for those who acknowledge your power and justice;
  they live in fear of punishment and retribution.
I pray for those who view you as their sovereign;
  they live to please you but are weary of the effort.
My prayer is that every person born into this world
  will discover the joy of being your beloved child
    and not simply a servant within your family.
Help me to embrace all my siblings—
  the servant and the one who rejoices in being your child—
    as truly loved and valued by you.
May I proclaim with joy that I live by faith,
  indeed, by the faithfulness of Christ,
    who loved me and gave himself for me. Amen.

Hymn:

Author of faith, eternal Word,
  Whose Spirit breathes the active flame,
Faith, like its finisher and Lord,
  Today as yesterday the same.

To you our humble hearts aspire,
  And ask the gift unspeakable:
Increase in us the kindled fire,
  In us the work of faith fulfill.

Faith lends its realizing light,
  The clouds disperse, the shadows fly;
The invisible appears in sight,
  And God is seen by mortal eye.

(Collection 92: 1, 2, 6)

33 ~
Reclaiming Our First Love

Scripture:

What more was there to do for my vineyard
  that I haven't done for it?
When I expected it to grow good grapes,
  why did it grow rotten grapes?

—Isaiah 5:4

Prayer:

Persevering God,
Straying from your path comes easy to us.
  We are so easily distracted by what surrounds us.
    Not all interruptions are bad, just diverting.
Keep us deeply rooted in the substance of our faith:
    a people of one book—the Bible,
    a fellowship that seeks the wisdom of the ages,
    a community that honors tradition,
    a cohort of pilgrims seeking the way of salvation.

Keep us intently focused on the spiritual wisdom of Jesus' way:
a vision of salvation by grace through faith,
a practice of life together in community,
a discipline of fellowship in intimate circles of friends,
an immersion in all the means of grace.

Keep us consistently conformed to a rule of life:
an avoidance of all known sin,
a commitment to doing good at all times,
a devotion to those places where we meet you,
a pursuit of the goal of perfect love.

Keep us joyfully dedicated to our first love:
a life characterized by the fruits of the Spirit,
a life averse to the seduction of wealth and power,
a life grateful for the good gifts you lavishly bestow. Amen.

Hymn:

What could your Redeemer do
More than he has done for you?
To procure your peace with God,
Could he more than shed his blood?
After all his waste of love,
All his drawings from above,
Why will you your Lord deny?
Why will you resolve to die?

Can you doubt if God is love?
If to all God's mercies move?

Will you not God's word receive?
Will you not God's oath believe?
See, the suffering God appears!
Jesus weeps! Believe his tears!
Mingled with his blood they cry,
Why will you resolve to die?

(Collection 8: 1, 4)

34 ~

Wealth and God's Rule

Scripture:

> In fact, it's easier for a camel to squeeze through the eye of a needle than for a rich person to enter God's kingdom.
>
> —*Matthew 19:24*

Prayer:

God of the Poor,
If I possess more than I absolutely need to live,
then I am rich.
If I have more food and clothing than I absolutely need,
then I am wealthy.
Nothing hinders growth in holiness like wealth;
wealth opens the door to all kinds of temptations.
Wealth precludes having the mind of Christ
or walking in the way that Christ walked.
Faith is the root of all true religion;

those who are wealthy trust in their riches.
Love is the first fruit of genuine faith;
the wealthy love money more than you.
Love of neighbor springs from love of you;
the wealthy see their neighbors as competitors.
True humility springs from love of God and neighbor;
the wealthy excel in pride and arrogance.
Thoughtfulness and patience characterize the meek;
the wealthy think only of themselves.
Guard me against
a practical atheism rooted in riches;
a dangerous idolatry that worships money;
an attraction to the seductive aspects of wealth;
a quest for happiness in anything other than you.
Open my eyes to the self-absorption and triviality
that characterize the life of the wealthy.
May I seek happiness in you and you alone. Amen.

Hymn:

Jesus, all-atoning Lamb,
Thine, and only thine I am;
Take my body, spirit, soul,
Only thou possess the whole!

Thou my one thing needful be;
Let me ever cleave to thee;
Let me choose the better part;
Let me give thee all my heart.

All my treasure is above;
All my riches is thy love.
Who the worth of love can tell?
Infinite, unsearchable!
(Collection 422: 1, 2, 5)

35

Free Grace

Scripture:

He didn't spare his own Son but gave him up for us all.
Won't he also freely give us all things with him?

—Romans 8:32

Prayer:

God of free grace,
your gracious love is all in all.
Your grace is a free gift in all.
It does not depend on
my power or merit,
my good works or righteousness,
my character, purposes, or intentions.
All these flow from the gift of your grace.
They are the streams only, not the fountain.
They are the fruits of free grace, not the root.
They are the effects of grace, not the cause.

I praise you, O God of free grace,
because your grace is a free gift in all.
Your grace is a free gift for all.
If you intended this gift only for a select few,
for those you chose for salvation,
I would have no use for the means of grace,
no incentive to grow in grace,
no sense of mutuality in love,
no need to put love into action,
and, ultimately, no need for Jesus.
I praise you, O God of free grace,
because your grace is a free gift for all.
I praise you, O God of free grace,
because you take no pleasure in the spiritual death of any.
You offer your grace as a free gift in all and for all.
Amen.

Hymn:

Your ceaseless, unexhausted love,
Unmerited and free,
Delights our evil to remove,
And help our misery.

You linger to be gracious still,
You do with sinners bear,
That saved we may your goodness feel,
And all your grace declare.

Its streams the whole creation reach,
    So plenteous is the store,
Enough for all, enough for each,
    Enough for evermore!

(Collection 241: 1, 2, 4)

36

A Christlike Life

Scripture:

Observe those who have integrity
 and watch those whose heart is right
because the future belongs to persons of peace.

—Psalm 37:37

Prayer:

Lord,
I want to be a Christian in my heart.
 I want your peace to fill my soul.
Grant me a Christlike spirit:
 May I believe in the name of Jesus Christ.
 May I live by faith in the Son of God.
 May your Spirit witness to me that I belong to you.
 May your Spirit shed abroad your love in my heart.
 May I love others as I love myself.
 May I have the mind that was in Christ.

May I be holy as Christ is holy.
May my conscience be void of offense to you.
May I be zealous for good works.
May I pursue one rule, to do all things to your glory.
Grant me a heart filled with peace:
an inward peace that passes all understanding,
an unspeakable calmness and serenity of spirit,
a tranquility rooted in a deep trust in your love,
a calmness of mind and imagination,
a blessed abiding in you at the approach of death,
a love that radiates your light.
I want to be a Christian in my heart.
I want your peace to fill my soul.
Keep my heart and mind safe in Christ Jesus. Amen.

Hymn:

Find in Christ the way of peace,
Peace unspeakable, unknown;
By his pain he gives you ease,
Life by his expiring groan;
Rise exalted by his fall,
Find in Christ your all in all.

O believe the record true,
God to you the Son has given!
You may now be happy too,
Live on earth the life of heaven;
Live the life of heaven above,
All the life of glorious love.

(Collection 20: 2, 3)

37

What Are Human Beings?

Scripture:

What are human beings
  that you think about them;
what are human beings
  that you pay attention to them?

—Psalm 8:4

Prayer:

Loving Creator,
We give thanks to you
  because we are marvelously and wondrously made.
You created our bodies.
  You formed us out of the elements of the universe,
    properly proportioned and mysteriously combined.
  The intricacy, complexity, and interconnectedness
    inspire our awe and lead us to marvel at your design.
  We thank you for our bodies,

but there is something more.
You created us with the ability to think.
We see, smell, hear, taste, and feel
and are able to judge, reason, and reflect.
We thank you for our minds,
but there is something more.
You created us with the capacity to love.
We experience joy, sorrow, desire, fear, and hope.
The soul is an inward principle that governs the whole.
Liberty characterizes the soul.
We have the power to choose good or ill,
to serve the benefit of others or ourselves.
We thank you for our souls.
In your great wisdom, O God, you created all things,
and you created us in your own image and likeness.
We give thanks to you for our bodies, minds, and souls.
They enable us to know, love, enjoy, and serve you forever. Amen.

Hymn:

You love all that your hands have made;
Your goodness we rehearse,
In shining characters displayed
Throughout our universe.

Mercy, with love, and endless grace
O'er all your works we find;
But mostly you delight to bless
Beloved humankind.

Therefore, let every creature give
  To you the praise designed;
But chiefly, Lord, our thanks receive,
  For hearts with yours aligned.
(Collection 229: 6, 7, 8)

38
Living by Faith

Scripture:

We live by faith and not by sight.

—2 Corinthians 5:7

Prayer:

God of the Way,
We live by faith and not by sight.
This is such a short but full description
of what it means to be a real Christian.
As true Christian believers,
we are not only your servants;
we are your beloved children.
We have the Spirit of adoption
crying in our hearts,
"Abba, Father."
You have brought us to life—abundant life—
and given us new senses, spiritual senses,

by the gift of faith given to us by the Spirit.
We walk by faith and not by sight.
Your gift of faith does for us
what neither sight nor any of the senses can do.
Help us to live by faith:
to see the hope of your call,
to embrace this new and living way,
to love those things that endure,
to serve those people who simply long for love.
Teach us that true religion is not about
right doctrine or morality, purity or formality.
True religion means to live in eternity—
to walk in the love of God and neighbor. Amen.

Hymn:

Forever here my rest shall be,
Close to your bleeding side;
This all my hope, and all my plea—
For me the Savior died!

Wash me, and make me thus your own;
Wash me, and never then depart;
Wash me, but not my feet alone—
My hands, my head, my heart.

Your grace and mercy now apply
Till faith to sight improve,
Till hope in full fruition die,
And all my soul be love.
(Collection 337: 1, 3, 4)

39 ~
A Litany

Scripture:

God is one.

—Mark 12:32

Prayer:

From everlasting to everlasting, you are—the great I Am.
We praise you, O God.
You fill all time and space with your glorious presence.
We praise you, O God.
You are perfect in every way—perfect in love.
We praise you, O God.
You know all things and watch over us with great care.
We praise you, O God.
You are Light, and in you, there is no darkness at all.
We praise you, O God.
You are a Spirit—parent of the spirits of all flesh.
We praise you, O God.

You made us for yourself; we are restless apart from you.
We praise you, O God.
You long for us to be happy, here, now, and forever.
We praise you, O God.
You are Alpha and Omega, the beginning and the end.
We praise you, O God.
You created us in your own image—the image of love—
may we all love you, therefore, with our whole heart,
and love everything else in you—our one, true God.
May it be so. Amen and amen.

Hymn:

Hail, holy, holy, holy Lord,
Whom One in Three we know;
By all your heavenly host adored,
By all your Church below.

One God, beneath, throughout, above,
With triumph we proclaim;
Your universe is full of love,
And speaks your glorious name.

Hail, holy, holy, holy Lord,
(Our heavenly song shall be),
Supreme, essential One, adored
In co-eternal Three!

(Collection 251: 1, 2, 6)

40

A Lament

Scripture:

Is there no balm in Gilead?
  Is there no physician there?
Why then have my people
  not been restored to health?

—Jeremiah 8:22

Prayer:

Forgiving God,
Why have we—your beloved children—
  failed to transform the world,
    to realize the peaceable rule of Christ?
Why do so many remain spiritually unhealthy,
  failing to display the mind that was in Christ
    or imitate his humility—his lowliness of heart?
    In your holy name, what are we doing?
Why are we not crucified to the world,
  dead to passionate desires and pride of life?

Why do we not walk as Christ walked?
Why do we gain all we can and save all we can,
but fail to give all we can,
leaving the poor even more desolate?
In your holy name, what are we doing?
Why do we impiously, unjustly, and cruelly
hoard material possessions for ourselves,
thereby robbing the poor of life's essentials?
Why do we turn our backs on the hungry
and those shivering from the cold
when we have more than we can ever use?
In your holy name, what are we doing?
Why have we failed to transform the world?
Because we have forgotten your solemn words:
"All who want to come after me must say no to themselves,
take up their cross daily and follow me."
Forgive us, merciful Lord. Amen.

Hymn:

Happy the souls that first believed,
To Jesus and each other cleaved,
Joined by the blessing from above
In mystic fellowship of love.

Where shall I wander now to find
Successors that they left behind?
The faithful, whom I seek in vain,
Seem banished from the world's domain.

(Collection 16: 1, 5)

41 ∾
Filled with Light

Scripture:

> If your eye is healthy, your whole body will be full of light.
>
> —*Matthew 6:22*

Prayer:

Illuminating God,
Two wings lift my soul to heaven:
    simplicity with regard to my intentions
        and purity with regard to my affections.
If I focus my intention and love on you,
    your Spirit lifts me into the light
        and you fill me with all holiness and happiness.
My soul soars when I think about what it means
    to be a real, inward, scriptural Christian,
        conformed in heart and life to your will and way.

Unless you birth my spirit anew,
I am destined to wander aimlessly in the darkness,
but my path is clear when you lift me to the light.
You draw me to the light and make all things possible:
if you are the singular focus of my attention,
you flood every part of me with light;
if you are my intention in all things great and small,
you fulfill all your wondrous promises in me;
if you are the One I seek to please above all others,
you frame my life with the radiance of love.
I praise you for the gift of your light.
When I am filled with this light,
I am able to rejoice evermore,
give thanks in all things, and pray unceasingly.
I am able to live with the knowledge
that you work all things together for good.
Thank you, O God, for the gift of light that fills my soul.
Amen.

Hymn:

Behold the servant of the Lord!
I wait your guiding eye to feel,
To hear and keep your every word,
To prove and do your perfect will;
Joyful from my own works to cease,
Glad to fulfill all righteousness.

Here then to you your own I leave;
Mold as you will the passive clay:

But let me all your stamp receive;
    But let me all your words obey;
Serve with a single heart and eye,
And to your glory live and die.

(Collection 417: 1, 4)

42

Putting on Christ

Scripture:

Friend, how did you get in here without wedding clothes?

—Matthew 22:12

Prayer:

Redemptive God,
We need new clothes!
We need to throw off the tatters we wear
and put on your magnificent robe of light.
We need to relinquish our sin and brokenness
and accept the glorious garment of pardon,
your greatest and most costly gift.
We need to put on the righteousness of Christ—
to worship you in the beauty of holiness
and live into the splendor of your love.
Open our hearts to your desire to renew our souls—

to restore the loving image of Christ in our lives.
Implant in our hearts a faith that works by love.
You are willing to save all the souls you have made.
You have prepared a realm of peace and joy for us all.
But you force none of us to accept this great gift.
You set before us all a choice between life and death.
You cry out, "Be holy and be happy, here and forever."
You call us to a banquet of light with the saints,
and your banner over us is love.
Clothed in our wedding garments, we come;
we come clothed with Christ,
loved, radiant, and joyfully expectant. Amen.

Hymn:

God of all-sufficient grace,
My God in Christ thou art;
Bid me walk before thy face,
Till I am pure in heart;
Till transformed by faith divine,
I gain that perfect love unknown,
Bright in all thine image shine,
By putting on thy Son.

Father, Son, and Holy Ghost,
In counsel join again
To restore thine image, lost
In fallenness and pain;
O might I thy form express,

Through faith begotten from above,
Stamped with real holiness,
And filled with perfect love!
(Collection 357: 3, 4)

43 ~
Treasure in Clay Pots

Scripture:

But we have this treasure in clay pots.

—2 Corinthians 4:7

Prayer:

Glorious God,
I am such a riddle to myself;
my life is such a strange set of inconsistencies:
a paradoxical mixture of good and evil,
eminence and insignificance,
nobility and desolation.
The more I reflect on this great mystery,
the more confused and entangled I become.
I take solace in your own words:
"Let us make humanity in our image to resemble us."
You are the source of my dignity and my value.

Help me to understand myself more fully.
I am your treasure:
You have given me a spiritual nature.
You have blessed me with understanding.
You have entrusted me with a conscience.
You have shed your love abroad in my heart.
You have gifted me with peace, joy, and love.
I carry this treasure, however, in a vulnerable clay pot.
I am weak and easily broken.
I am rebellious and defiant.
My judgment is poor.
My mistakes are countless.
All I can do is pray: "Not to me, Lord,
but to your own name give glory,
because of your loyal love and faithfulness!" Amen.

Hymn:

Our life is hid with Christ in God;
Our life shall soon appear,
And shed his glory all abroad
In all his members here.

This heavenly treasure now we have
In a vile house of clay:
But Christ shall to the utmost save,
And keep it to that day.

Then let us hasten to the day
    When all shall be brought home!
Come, O Redeemer, come away!
    O Jesus, quickly come!
        (Collection 523: 7, 8, 13)

44 ~
An Intercession

Scripture:

In this world you had no hope and no God.

—*Ephesians 2:12*

Prayer:

Patient God,
We pray today for those who do not know you,
  who struggle to live life without you.
    Oh why should they wander as aliens from you?
    They cry in the desert to hear your voice!
We pray for those who have no companionship with you.
  Open their hearts to your loving presence.
We pray for those who cannot see you.
  Open their eyes to light and love.
We pray for those who have never heard your call.
  Open their ears to the voice of the Good Shepherd.
We pray for those who have no spiritual sense.

Open their souls to the power of your love.
We pray for those who are fixated on their wounds.
Open their bodies to the healing balm of the Spirit.
We pray for those who struggle to break free.
Open their lives to the new creation you provide.
Hear us, Lord, speak to each of your beloved children
and penetrate their hearts with your message of hope:
"Arise, shine, Your light has come;
My glory has shone upon you.
Though darkness covers the earth
I will shine upon you." Amen.

Hymn:

Thee without faith I cannot please:
Faith without thee I cannot have:
But thou hast sent the Prince of Peace
To seek my wandering soul, and save:
O Father! Glorify thy Son,
And save me for his sake alone!

Save me through faith in Jesus' blood,
That blood which he for all did shed:
For me, for me, thou knowest, it flowed,
For me, for me thou hearest it plead;
Assure me now my soul is thine,
And all thou art in Christ is mine!
(Redemption Hymns 14: 4, 5)

45

The Danger of Increasing Riches

Scripture:

When wealth bears fruit,
don't set your heart on it.

—Psalm 62:10

Prayer:

God of the Poor,
We repent of our addiction to affluence.
Wealth simply makes us want more—
more money, more power, more control.
We acknowledge that these desires
are antithetical to the way of Jesus
and blind us to the plight of our neighbor.
Instead of empathy for those on the margins,
we offer pity at best and apathy at worst,
and disregard our suffering siblings.
Forgive us, we pray, when we fail to hear
the cry of the needy.

We repent of our addiction to affluence.
It is so easy for us to deceive ourselves
and conclude that we have so little.
We say in self-satisfaction, "I am not rich.
So many others have so much more than I.
I must keep this or that for myself."
We are drawn into the downward spiral of selfishness,
placing self-interest above the needs of others
and putting our faith in what we possess.
Forgive us, we pray, when we fail to love
our neighbors as we love ourselves.
Convict us when we set our hearts
on the increase of our wealth
at the peril of our souls. Amen.

Hymn:

We have laid up our love
And treasure above,
Though our bodies continue below;
The redeemed of the Lord,
We remember God's word,
And with singing to paradise go.

With singing we praise
The original grace
By our heavenly Father bestowed;
Our being receive
From God's bounty, and live
To the honor and glory of God.

(Collection 478: 2, 3)

46 ~
The Prospect of Heaven

Scripture:

Now faith is the substance of things hoped for, the evidence of things not seen.

—Hebrews 11:1 (KJV)

Prayer:

Eternal God,
Faith means trust—trust in you and trust in your ways.
Faith has to do with spiritual realities unseen,
  with intangibles that give life meaning.
But faith also governs the reality of death
  and provides a vision of eternal life with you.
No eye has seen, nor ear heard,
  nor the human heart conceived,
    what you have prepared for those who love you.
The prospect of heaven is thrilling, O God:
    eternal holiness and happiness for the faithful;

enlivened conversation with wise and holy souls;
harmonious sounds of angels and archangels in song;
communion with Christ in whom all wisdom resides.

The prospect of heaven is thrilling, O God:
swallowed up in your infinite love;
comprehending the whole immensity of space;
celebrating your presence, above, beneath, all around;
moving as swift as thought.

The prospect of heaven is thrilling, O God:
surveying your works of creation and providence,
increasing moment by moment in wisdom and knowledge,
experiencing and rejoicing in the power of love,
proclaiming your holiness with the whole company of heaven.

The prospect of heaven is thrilling, Eternal God!
We long for that time when the invisible appears in sight and we see you in glory face to face. Amen.

Hymn:

The spirit of interceding grace
Give us in faith to claim,
To wrestle till we see your face,
And know your hidden name.

I will not let you go, unless
You tell your name to me;

With all your great salvation bless—
    Through faith my heart set free.

Then let me on the mountain top
    Behold your open face,
Where faith in sight is swallowed up,
    And prayer in endless praise.
(Collection 288: 3, 5, 6)

47 ৵
Seek First the Kingdom

Scripture:

> Instead, desire first and foremost God's kingdom and God's righteousness, and all these things will be given to you as well.
>
> —*Matthew 6:33*

Prayer:

Sovereign God,
I worry so much about my life,
    what I'll eat and what I'll drink,
        about my body and what to wear.
I know that life is more than food
    and the body more than clothes,
        but I get trapped in cycles of worry.
I know that worrying adds nothing to my life.
    You know exactly what I need,

so why do I lose sleep over life's worries?
I pray for a desire first and foremost for your kingdom.
The righteousness to which you call me
is lovely and pure;
The joy you seek to cultivate in me
is indelible, precious, and eternal.
The peace into which you invite me
is characterized by "perfect love."
If I seek your rule in my life above all else,
you promise to give me all these things as well.
All honor, majesty, and dominion
be ascribed to you, ever-blessed Trinity—
both now and forevermore. Amen.

Hymn:

I seek the kingdom first,
The gracious joy and peace,
You know, I hunger, Lord, and thirst
After your righteousness;
My chief, and sole desire
Your image to regain,
And then to join your heavenly choir,
And with your children reign.

My God will add the rest,
Will outward good provide:
But with your kingdom in my breast,
I nothing want beside:
Glory begun in grace

Delightfully I prove,
And earth and heaven at once possess
In all-sufficient love.

(Scripture Hymns, vol. 2,
Matthew, 74, 75)

48

The Promise of Understanding

Scripture:

> You don't understand what I'm doing now, but you will understand later.
>
> *—John 13:7*

Prayer:

All-wise God,
Your ways are not my ways.
So much of what you do remains hidden;
what I do see often remains a mystery.
How you threw the stars into the heavens,
or regulate the planets in their courses,
or govern 100 billion galaxies escapes me.
How you created me,
weaving my unique soul with my body,
boggles my mind and stretches my imagination.
All I can say is that the mystery who is you

engages the mystery who is me,
and the bond that holds us together is your love.
I cannot even fully understand
this prayer that I pray to you now.
How does prayer even work?
I am left with so many questions:
Why does evil have a place in your creation?
Why do some embody virtue with such apparent ease?
Why are others caught in cycles of violence and suffering?
Why do some use their gifts for the benefit of others?
Why do others abuse power and grasp at personal gain?
But my inability to comprehend your whole design
keeps me humble and teachable, open and inquisitive.
I await the promise of understanding
when I am pure and strong enough to see you
and dwell in the light no mortal can approach!
Amen.

Hymn:

Do what you will; it *should* be so:
Your works I shall hereafter know,
(When death the veil remove)
Unwind the providential maze,
And gladly own that all your ways
Are wisdom, truth, and love.

(Scripture Hymns, vol. 2, John, 451)

49

The Image of God

Scripture:

God created humanity in God's own image.

—*Genesis 1:27*

Prayer:

Wise Creator,
We praise you for creating us in your image.
Our view of ourselves and our vision of life begins here.
Your desire has always been for all your children
to reflect your beauty, goodness, and love.
To be created in your image means
to have the ability to understand—to perceive truth.
To be created in your image means
to have the ability to act—to choose the good.
To be created in your image means
to have the ability to love—to share true happiness.
You created us in your image and likeness,

and because we are like you,
we seek to be you—we want to be God.
Ironically, this is our fatal flaw.
Our pride becomes the ultimate paradox of our existence—
the greatest impediment to our happiness—
instead of loving you, we love ourselves.
We ask in all humility for you to restore your image in us;
only you can restore what our pride has defaced.
We ask you to restore our understanding and our will
so we can reflect the beauty and goodness you intend.
Most important, we ask you to order our loves properly,
to fill our whole being with your self-giving love,
and for that love to possess us without rival.
You intended your love to be the core of our being.
Restore your image in us; radiate that love through us.
Amen.

Hymn:

The Ancient of Days
To redeem a lost race,
From great glory comes down,
Self-humbled to carry us up to a crown.

Made flesh for our sake,
That we might partake
The nature divine,
And again in Christ's image, God's holiness shine.

And while we are here,
Our Lord shall appear,
The Spirit impart,
And form God's full image of love in our heart.

(Nativity Hymns 8: 4, 5, 8)

50

The Love of God

Scripture:

> You must love the Lord your God with all your heart, with all your being, with all your mind, and with all your strength.
>
> —*Mark 12:30*

Prayer:

Loving God,
You formed me out of the dust of the earth
  and breathed the breath of life into me.
You stamped your image upon me
  in my understanding, will, and affections.
You commanded me to love you
  in order to perfect my own happiness.
Whenever I turn my back on you,
  you seek every opportunity to restore me.

My holiness and my happiness
are your singular concern.
Love is the end of every command of Christ,
the purpose of which is to put love
at the center of everything I am and do.
I want to love you with my whole being:
to delight in you and express my gratitude to you,
to devote to you the highest degree of my love,
to define all my loves in reference to you.
I want my nature and my name to be love, like you:
to love all people without condition,
to love everything and everyone you have made,
to love in a way that reflects your unbounded love.
Unto you, O God, who first loved me,
unto you, O Christ, who received and restored me,
unto you, O Holy Spirit, who fills my heart with love,
be all love and all glory, now and forevermore.
Amen.

Hymn:

To love is all my wish,
I only live for this:
Grant me, Lord, my heart's desire,
There by faith forever dwell.
This I always will require,
Thee and only thee to feel.

Ah! Give me this to know,
With all thy saints below;

Swells my soul to compass thee;
    Gasps in thee to live and move,
Filled with all the Deity,
    All immersed and lost in love!
(Collection 26: 4, 6)

51 ~

The One Thing Necessary

Scripture:

One thing is necessary.

—Luke 10:42

Prayer:

Parent of All Good,
I come to you with a heavy heart.
I have squandered your good gifts,
forgotten your deep love,
abandoned your dream for my life.
I have put myself first, even above you.
I confess that I am fallen and need you so desperately.
I am so far from what you want me to be.
You surround me with your light,
but I remain lost in the darkness still.
Therefore, restore your image of love in me;
that is the only thing I truly need.

You created me for this one end—to love you.
You redeemed me for this one end—to dwell in love.
You continue to work within me for this one end—
to perfect my love for you and others.

Love is your very image, the brightness of your glory.
Love not only makes me like you; love makes me one with you.
Fulfill, then, Jesus' vision for me and all your children:
"Whoever loves me will keep my word.
My Father will love them,
and we will come to them
and make our home with them."
Make your home in my heart, beloved Lover of my soul. Amen.

Hymn:

Ever fainting with desire,
For thee, O Christ, I call!
Thee I restlessly require,
I want my God, my all.
Jesus, dear redeeming Lord,
I want thy coming from above:
Help me, Savior, speak the word,
And perfect me in love.

Thou, my life, my treasure be,
My portion here below!
Nothing would I seek but thee,
Thee only would I know,
My exceeding great reward,

My heaven on earth, my heaven above:
Help me, Savior, speak the word,
And perfect me in love.

(Collection 344: 1, 5)

52
A Canticle of Love

Scripture:

If I give away everything that I have and hand over my own body to feel good about what I've done but I don't have love, I receive no benefit whatsoever.

—1 Corinthians 13:3

Prayer:

God of Love,
We delight in you, rejoice in your will,
desire continually to please you,
and seek our happiness in you.
We thirst day and night for a fuller enjoyment of you.
We are lost in wonder, love, and praise.
We will seek to love our neighbors for your sake:
If they are in error, we will restore, not reproach them.

If they provoke us, we will respond with gentleness.
We are lost in wonder, love, and praise.

We will seek to be kind in all our thoughts and actions:
We will speak with tenderness and empathy.
We will act for the happiness of all people.
We are lost in wonder, love, and praise.

We will seek humility in all we think and do:
All we have and all we are is yours, loving God.
The good we do is rooted in the power of love.
We are lost in wonder, love, and praise.

We will seek to love because love comes from you:
We praise you for your pure, unbounded love.
We love because you first loved us.
We are lost in wonder, love, and praise. Amen.

Hymn:

Love divine, all loves excelling,
Joy of heaven, to earth come down,
Fix in us thy humble dwelling,
All thy faithful mercies crown!
Jesu, thou art all compassion,
Pure, unbounded love thou art;
Visit us with thy salvation!
Enter every trembling heart.

Finish then thy new creation,
Pure and spotless let us be;
Let us see thy great salvation
Perfectly restored in thee;

Changed from glory into glory,
  Till in heaven we take our place,
Till we cast our crowns before thee,
  Lost in wonder, love, and praise.
(Collection 374: 1, 3)

Wesley's Original Sermon Titles

The original titles and the sermon number in parentheses (under which Wesley's sermons are published in *The Works of John Wesley,* volumes 1-4) appear below with the titles used in this volume in *italics.*

1. On Eternity (54) (*The Eternal God*)
2. On the Trinity (55) (*The Holy Trinity*)
3. God's Approbation of His Works (56) (*God's Love of All Creation*)
4. God's Love to Fallen Man (59) (*God's Free Gift*)
5. The End of Christ's Coming (62) (*The Mission of Christ*)
6. The General Spread of the Gospel (63) (*Love Is on the Move*)
7. The New Creation (64) (*New Creation*)
8. On Divine Providence (67) (*God's Providential Care*)
9. The Wisdom of God's Counsels (68) (*The Wisdom of God*)
10. Of the Church (74) (*The Community of Faith*)
11. On Schism (75) (*Lamenting Christian Division*)
12. On Perfection (76) (*Christian Maturity*)
13. Spiritual Worship (77) (*Spiritual Worship*)

14. On Temptation (82) (*On Temptation*)
15. On Patience (83) (*On Patience*)
16. The Important Question (84) (*The Important Question*)
17. On Working Out Our Own Salvation (85) (*On Working Out Our Own Salvation*)
18. The Danger of Riches (87) (*The Danger of Riches*)
19. On Dress (88) (*The Simple Life*)
20. The More Excellent Way (89) (*The More Excellent Way*)
21. An Israelite Indeed (90) (*Authenticity*)
22. On Charity (91) (*Humble Love*)
23. On Zeal (92) (*On Zeal*)
24. On Redeeming the Time (93) (*Self-Care*)
25. On Family Religion (94) (*Family Religion*)
26. On the Education of Children (95) (*Spiritual Formation*)
27. On Visiting the Sick (98) (*Compassion in Action*)
28. The Reward of Righteousness (99) (*The Christlike Servant*)
29. On Pleasing All Men (100) (*Building Each Other Up*)
30. The Duty of Constant Communion (101) (*Constant Communion*)
31. On Conscience (105) (*A Good Conscience*)
32. On Faith (106) (*On Faith*)
33. On God's Vineyard (107) (*Reclaiming Our First Love*)
34. On Riches (108) (*Wealth and God's Rule*)
35. Free Grace (110) (*Free Grace*)
36. On the Death of John Fletcher (114) (*A Christlike Life*)
37. What is Man? (116) (*What Are Human Beings?*)
38. Walking by Sight and Walking by Faith (119) (*Living by Faith*)
39. The Unity of the Divine Being (120) (*A Litany*)

Scripture Index of Sermon Texts

THE OLD TESTAMENT (Hebrew Scriptures)

Scripture Text	*Sermon Number*
Genesis 1:27	49
Genesis 1:31	3
Joshua 24:15	25
Psalm 8:4	37
Psalm 37:37	36
Psalm 62:10	45
Psalm 90:2	1
Proverbs 22:6	26
Isaiah 5:4	33
Isaiah 11:9	6
Jeremiah 8:22	40

THE NEW TESTAMENT

Scripture Text	*Sermon Number*
Matthew 6:22	41
Matthew 6:33	47
Matthew 16:26	16
Matthew 19:24	34

Index of Hymns

In the following index, the hymn selections are placed in numerical sequence as they appear in the 1780 *Collection of Hymns for the Use of the People called Methodists.* The numbers following the colon indicate the stanzas of the hymn. At the conclusion of each hymn excerpt in the readings above, all hymn number and stanza references come from this collection. Selections from other hymn sources are noted at the conclusion of the index as well as following the respective hymns above, using their abbreviations.

Hymn Sources:

Hildebrandt, Franz and Beckerlegge, Oliver, eds. *The Works of John Wesley. Volume 7. A Collection of Hymns for the Use of the People called Methodists.* Nashville: Abingdon Press, 1983.

Funeral Hymns

Wesley, Charles. *Funeral Hymns.* London: Strahan, 1759.

Nativity Hymns

Wesley, Charles Wesley. *Hymns for the Nativity of our Lord.* London: Strahan, 1745.

Redemption Hymns

Wesley, Charles. *Hymns for Those that Seek and Those that Have Redemption in the Blood of Jesus Christ*. London: Strahan, 1747.

Scripture Hymns

Wesley, Charles. *Short Hymns on Select Passages of the Holy Scriptures*. 2 vols. Bristol: Farley, 1762.

Hymn	*First Line*	*Sermon*
2: 1, 2, 3	Come, sinners, to the gospel feast	30
8: 1, 4	What could your Redeemer do	33
14: 1, 2, 5	Happy the man that's find the grace	21
16: 1, 5	Happy the souls that first believed	40
20: 2, 3	Weary souls that wander wide	36
26: 4, 6	Saviour, the world's and mine	50
39: 1, 2 7	O God, our help in ages past	1
66: 6, 8	How happy is the pilgrim's lot	18
92: 1, 2, 6	Author of faith, eternal Word	32
142: 2, 3	Father of Jesus Christ the just	7
207: 6, 8, 9	Infinite, unexhausted Love	22
216: 1, 3, 6	Praise ye the Lord! 'tis good to raise	3
225: 1, 3	Father of all, whose powerful voice	8
229: 6, 7, 8	Hail, Father, Son, and Holy Ghost	37
235: 1, 3	Thou, the great eternal Lord	9
236: 1, 2	Good you art, and good thou dost	4
241: 1, 2, 4	Thy ceaseless, unexhausted love	35
251: 1, 2, 6	Holy, holy, holy, holy Lord	39
288: 3, 5, 6	Shepherd divine, our wants relive	46

Hymn	*First Line*	*Sermon*
291: 1, 2	Jesus, I fain would find	23
292: 1, 3	Jesu, my strength, my hope	14
292: 5, 6	Jesu, my strength, my hope	15
299: 1, 2, 3	I want a principle within	31
334: 1, 4, 8	O for a heart to praise my God	12
335: 1, 4	Thou hidden love of God, whose height	13
337: 1, 3, 4	Forever here my rest shall be	38
344: 1, 5	Ever fainting with desire	51
357: 3, 4	Father, see this living clod	42
374: 1, 3	Love divine, all loves excelling	52
401: 1, 2	Once thou didst on earth appear	5
417: 1, 4	Behold the servant of the Lord	41
418: 1, 4	Father, Son, and Holy Ghost	2
419: 5, 6	O God, what offering shall I give	19
421: 1, 3	Give me the faith which can remove	24
422: 1, 2, 5	Jesus, all-atoning Lamb	34
422: 4, 6, 7	Jesus, all-atoning Lamb	16
423: 1, 2, 6	Father, to thee my soul I lift	17
436: 2, 3	Prince of universal peace	6
460: 1, 4	I and my house will serve the Lord	25
461:1, 5	Come, Father, Son, and Holy Ghost	26
478: 2, 3	Come away to the skies	45
482: 1, 3	Come let us arise	27
501: 1, 3, 4	Father, Son, and Holy Spirit, hear	10
504: 7, 9, 10	Christ, from whom all blessings flow	11
507: 1, 2a	Let us join ('tis God commands)	20
523: 7, 8, 13	God of all consolation, take	43

Hymn	*First Line*	*Sermon*
Funeral Hymns 32: 2, 3	Mercy that heaven-descending guest	28
Nativity Hymns 8: 4, 5, 8	Away with our fears	49
Redemption Hymns 14: 4, 5	Father of Jesus Christ the just	44
Redemption Hymns 32: 1, 3a	All praise to our redeeming Lord	29
Scripture Hymns, vol. 2, Matt., 74, 75	I seek the kingdom first	47
Scripture Hymns, vol. 2, John, 451	Do what thou wilt; it should be so	48

About the Author

PAUL W. CHILCOTE, now in retirement, served most recently as Director of the Centre for Global Wesleyan Theology at Wesley House, Cambridge, where he remains a Fellow. A Methodist historian and theologian, he was involved in theological education on three continents, having taught at Wesley College Bristol & Wesley House Cambridge (England), St. Paul's United Theological College (Kenya), the Methodist Theological School (Ohio), Duke Divinity School (North Carolina), Ashland Theological Seminary (Ohio), and having helped launch two new institutions – Africa University (Zimbabwe) and Asbury Theological Seminary (Florida). He is an award-winning author and editor of nearly forty books, including *Praying in the Wesleyan Spirit, Recapturing the Wesleys' Vision, A Faith That Sings, The Methodist Defense of Women in Ministry, Making Disciples in a World Parish, Early Methodist Spirituality, Active Faith, Living Hope, Singing the Faith,* and *Multiplying Love.* He is a frequent speaker and workshop leader in applied Wesleyan studies, particularly in the areas of theology, spirituality, and Christian discipleship. He has been a Benedictine oblate of Mt. Angel Abbey for over twenty-five years. He and his wife, Janet, a retired United Methodist pastor, have five daughters, Sandy, Rebekah, Anna, Mary, and Ruth, and seven grandchildren, Alyssa, Levi, and Theo Brooks, Collin, Oliver, and Elsie Glass, and Isabella Gitonga.